A Kid's Guide to Drawing the Countries of the World™

How to Draw
Pakistan's
Sights and Symbols

Cindy Fazzi

The Rosen Publishing Group's
PowerKids Press™
New York

To my husband, Vincent, just for being you

Published in 2005 by The Rosen Publishing Group, Inc.
29 East 21st Street, New York, NY 10010

First Edition

Editor: Rachel O'Connor
Book Design: Kim Sonsky
Layout Design: Mike Donnellan

Illustration Credits: Cover and inside by Holly Cefrey.
Photo Credits: Cover and title page (hand) © Arlan Dean; p. 5 © AFP/CORBIS; p. 9 © Keren Su/CORBIS; p. 10 © Roger Wood/CORBIS; p. 13 A.R. Faridi Art Gallery, Karachi Arts Council; p. 16 (flag) © Eyewire; pp. 16 (coin), 18 © Rosen Publishing; p. 20 © Richard Shiell/Animals Animals; p. 22 © W. Wayne Lockwood, M.D./CORBIS; p. 24 © David Fritts/Animals Animals; p. 26 © Royalty Free/CORBIS; p. 28 © Paul Almasy/CORBIS; p. 30 © Ric Ergenbright/CORBIS; pp. 32, 36 © Diego Lezama Orezzoli/CORBIS; p. 34 © Robert Holmes/CORBIS; p. 38 © Bradley Mayhew/Lonely Planet Images; p. 40 © J A Giordano/CORBIS SABA; p. 42 © CORBIS.

Thanks to Syed Yawar Mehdi, General Secretary, Karachi Arts Council

Library of Congress Cataloging-in-Publication Data

Fazzi, Cindy.
How to draw Pakistan's sights and symbols / Cindy Fazzi.— 1st ed.
    p. cm. — (A Kid's guide to drawing the countries of the world)
Summary: Discusses the history, geography, plants and animals, culture, architecture and sights, and more of Pakistan. Provides guides to drawing features and symbols of the country.
Includes bibliographical references and index.
ISBN 1-4042-2739-3 (Library Binding)
1. Drawing—Technique—Juvenile literature. 2. Pakistan—In art—Juvenile literature. [1. Pakistan. 2. Drawing—Technique. 3. Pakistan—In art.] I. Title. II. Series.
NC655.F377 2005
743'.8995491—dc22

                                    2003020972

Manufactured in the United States of America

CONTENTS

Let's Draw Pakistan

The history of Pakistan goes back as far as the Indus Valley civilization. Around 2500–1500 B.C., a group of people called Dravidians lived in the Indus Valley in what today is known as Pakistan and northwestern India. In 1700 B.C., a nomadic tribe called the Aryans came to the Indus Valley from central Asia. The Aryans brought with them the four books called Vedas, which form the basis of Hinduism. The Aryans were replaced by Muslim invaders. Muslims practice the Islamic faith, which was founded by the prophet Muhammad.

For much of its history, Pakistan was a part of India. In 1206, most of Pakistan was under the rule of the Delhi Sultanate, a Muslim empire in India. The empire ended in 1526, when Bābur, a Muslim ruler from central Asia, invaded India and founded the Mughal Empire. The Mughals brought prosperity because they controlled many sources of spices and jewels. This attracted European traders in the 1600s, including the British. The British became

Most of the people living in Pakistan today are Muslims. Every Friday, Muslims gather to pray. Here, thousands of Muslim worshipers attend Friday prayers at a mosque in the city of Lahore, in eastern Pakistan.

more involved in India and finally took control of the country in 1857. The area they controlled, which included Pakistan, was known as British India. Under British rule, many Hindus went to British schools, and Muslims attended their own schools. As a result, the Hindus got good jobs. The Muslims remained poor.

In 1940, a group called the Muslim League demanded a homeland for Muslims in India. The group wanted to call its homeland Pakistan. Mohammed Ali Jinnah was the league's leader. The British and the Hindus rejected the league's demand. In 1946, a huge Muslim demonstration ended in bloody fighting between Muslims and Hindus. British and Hindu leaders agreed at last to divide India into Hindu and Muslim countries. On August 14, 1947, Pakistan became an independent Muslim nation.

Fighting continued between the Muslims and the Hindus even after the division of Pakistan and India. On top of this, the Muslims in Pakistan were divided. Those who lived in western Pakistan controlled the government and the military, which made the people in eastern Pakistan unhappy. By

1971, eastern Pakistan declared its independence and called itself Bangladesh. In spite of all the fighting, Pakistan survived, or lived on, and remains an independent country today. In this book you will learn more about Pakistan and how to draw some of the country's sights and symbols. Directions are under each step. New steps are shown in red. You will need the following supplies to draw Pakistan's sights and symbols:

- A sketch pad
- An eraser
- A number 2 pencil
- A pencil sharpener

These are some of the shapes and drawing terms you need to know to draw Pakistan's sights and symbols:

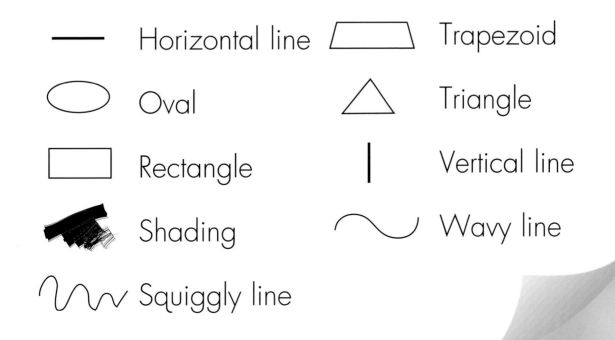

— Horizontal line   Trapezoid

Oval   Triangle

Rectangle | Vertical line

Shading   Wavy line

Squiggly line

More About Pakistan

Pakistan means "land of the pure" in Urdu, which is the country's national language. However, less than 10 percent of the people speak Urdu as their first language. More than 300 dialects are spoken throughout the country. Almost all Pakistanis are Muslims.

Pakistan has a population of 148 million people. The nation's capital is Islamabad, with a population of 901,137. Pakistan is a poor country. It has some industries, but it depends largely on agriculture. Most Pakistanis live in rural, or farming, areas. About 40 percent of the country's workers are in agriculture. The country's main crops are wheat, cotton, rice, sugarcane, fruits, and vegetables. Many farmers raise sheep and goats. Pakistan's fishermen sell shrimp, sardines, and sharks to other countries.

Pakistan has reserves of coal and petroleum, which provide for two-thirds of the country's energy needs. Pakistan's main industries are the production of clothing and textiles, food products, steel, and

The Indus River is Pakistan's most important river, and is the sixth-largest river system in the world. It stretches for 1,800 miles (2,897 km). The Indus River is pictured here as it flows through the Hunza Valley in the northwestern region of Pakistan.

cement. There are many Pakistanis who make carpets, pottery, and leather products from their homes or in small factories. These products are mostly exported, or sold in other countries.

Since Pakistan is a poor country, many people have left in search of better jobs overseas. Since the 1970s, hundreds of thousands of Pakistanis have gone to work in Saudi Arabia, Kuwait, Bahrain, Qatar, and the United Arab Emirates. These countries are rich because of their oil reserves. There are also many Pakistanis who live and work in Great Britain and the United States. Pakistan's government is trying to improve the economy by reducing Pakistan's debts to foreign countries and by increasing its exports.

Pakistan has faced many political problems from the time it became independent in 1947. It has gone through periods of military rule, when the army took over the government. Pakistan came back under military rule when General Pervez Musharraf named himself Pakistan's president in 2001.

In 2002, about 32 percent of the people of Pakistan were living in poverty and that poverty has increased in rural areas. Pictured here are three children in northern Pakistan.

The Artist
Ustad Allah Bukhsh

Allah Bukhsh (1895–1978) is one of Pakistan's most important painters. He is called Ustad, meaning "teacher," as a sign of respect for his great talent. He was born in Punjab, in central-eastern Pakistan, in 1895. It is not known whether he went to school to study art, but he started out as a painter of signs. Then he worked in the theater, where he painted scenes used as backgrounds for plays. In 1922, he painted his first picture of Lord Krishna, a god of the Hindu religion. The painting was sold within hours after he finished it. It was his first success. After that, he became famous as a painter of Lord Krishna.

In the 1920s, when Pakistan was still a part of India, Bukhsh displayed his paintings in many exhibitions throughout India. In 1923, he won the top prize in the exhibition of the Bombay Art Society. Bukhsh painted with oils and watercolors. His style of painting was European, but his subjects were his country and his people.

Aside from his paintings of Lord Krishna, Bukhsh is famous for painting scenes and characters from mythological, or made up, stories. He also painted

12

landscapes, such as mountains and rocks. By the late 1950s, Bukhsh's eyesight started to get weak. His last exhibition was held in 1976, in Karachi, a city in southern Pakistan. He died in 1978. Although Bukhsh's works show a part of Pakistan's history that is connected to India, Pakistanis have always been proud of his paintings.

Bukhsh was a quiet person. This quietness is reflected in his painting called *Landscape*, in which the trees and the surroundings are gentle and peaceful.

We do not know when Bukhsh painted this landscape of trees, because it is not dated. It is believed, however, that he became interested in landscape paintings in the 1940s. Bukhsh used oil on canvas for this painting, which measures 23" x 34" (58 cm x 86 cm).

Map of Pakistan

Map of the Continent of Asia

Pakistan is in southern Asia. India shares Pakistan's eastern border. Iran lies to the west, and Afghanistan is to the north. The Arabian Sea lies to the south. Pakistan has four provinces. These are Punjab, Sind, Baluchistan, and North-West Frontier. Pakistan also controls part of the state of Jammu and Kashmir, which is commonly known as Kashmir. Kashmir is located in the northern highlands between Pakistan and India. About two-thirds of Kashmir belongs to India, and one-third to Pakistan. The two countries continue to fight over ownership of Kashmir today. Pakistan is covered with mountains in the North and the West. This area is called the Northern and Western Highlands. The country has seven of the 16 tallest mountains in Asia and 40 of the world's 50 highest mountains.

1

Draw a horizontal and a vertical line that meet at a corner as shown. Draw another vertical and horizontal line inside the first lines, so that you have a square in the corner.

2

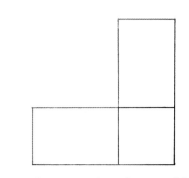

Add more horizontal and vertical lines as shown. You now have two rectangles and the square you drew in step 1. These will be your guides to drawing the map of Pakistan.

3

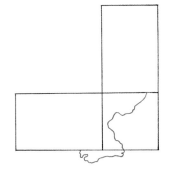

In the bottom square, draw the wavy line as shown. Notice how this line goes beyond the bottom horizontal guide. It should extend beneath the rectangle.

4

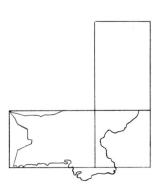

Continue this wavy line as shown in the bottom rectangle. You have now completed the southern part of Pakistan.

5

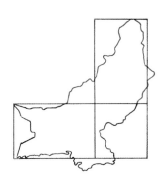

Complete the northern part of Pakistan by drawing the shape shown. Pay attention to where the line goes outside the guides.

6

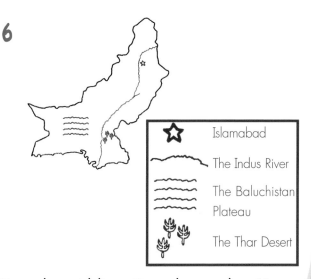

Islamabad

The Indus River

The Baluchistan Plateau

The Thar Desert

Erase the guidelines. Draw the map key. You can finish by shading your map and adding some of Pakistan's sights and symbols. Well done! You are finished drawing Pakistan.

Flag of Pakistan

Pakistan's flag is dark green with a white band on the left side. There is a white crescent, like a curved moon, and a five-pointed star in the middle. The Muslim League first adopted the crescent and star as its symbols in 1906. These are the traditional symbols of a Muslim country. The white stripe was added in 1947, after Pakistan became independent. It stands for the religious minorities in the country.

Currency of Pakistan

The rupee is the unit of currency in Pakistan. There are 100 paise to one rupee. The first coins of an independent Pakistan were issued in 1948. The coins bore English writing until 1964. The front of the coin shows how much the coin is worth. This coin is worth 25 paise.

Flag

1

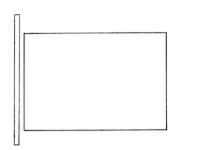

Draw the two rectangles as shown. One is long and thin. The other is wide and horizontal. These rectangles will be your guides.

2

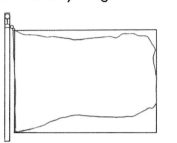

Draw a small circle at the top of the long, thin rectangle. Draw a small line as shown. Add two horizontal lines underneath the circle and line. Add two small circles that will connect the two rectangles. Draw the shape for the flag inside the large rectangle as shown.

3

Erase the large rectangle and the guidelines at the top of the flagpole. Draw the lines inside the flag as shown. Draw the moon crescent and a star.

4

Add details to the flagpole. You can finish your drawing with shading. The shading helps to give the effect of the wind blowing the flag. Well done. You have finished the Pakistan flag.

Currency

1

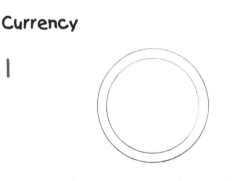

Begin by drawing two circles as shown.

2

Inside these two circles, draw a curved line at the bottom as shown. Draw a large 25 and add 1992 for the year underneath.

3

Draw the pattern on the curved line. Add the word "PAISE," and the squiggly shapes beside it. Draw small lines on the inner circle.

4

Erase the curved line. Continue the small lines all the way around the inside circle. Finish with shading.

Pakistan's National Emblem

Pakistan's national emblem symbolizes its people's religious beliefs and cultural heritage. On top of the emblem are the crescent and star,

the traditional symbols of Islam. In the middle is a shield with four divisions showing Pakistan's traditional crops. They are cotton, wheat, tea, and jute, which is a plant used to weave coarse cloth for sacks and bags. The wreath surrounding the shield is a design, or pattern, with flowers that is used in traditional Mughal art. It stands for Pakistan's cultural heritage. The Mughals were Muslims from central Asia who invaded India in 1526, when Pakistan was still a part of India.

At the bottom of the wreath is a scroll with writing that says "faith, unity, discipline" in Urdu. This is the motto of Mohammed Ali Jinnah, the founding father of Pakistan. It represents the country's guiding principles.

I

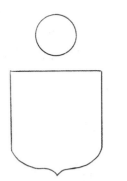

Draw a circle. Draw a shield as shown.

2

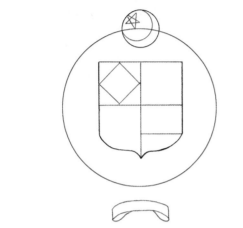

Draw a large circle. Draw a star in the small circle at the top. Draw a half circle inside this circle to make a crescent. Draw the lines inside the shield. Add a square shape that is on its point. Draw the shape below the shield.

3

Add curvy shapes to the side of the shape you have just drawn. This is the banner. Erase part of the small circle to leave the crescent and star. Erase the lines inside the star. Draw tea, cotton, wheat, and jute, featured inside the four compartments of the shield as shown. Draw the leaf detail on the large circle.

4

Finish the wreath that is surrounding the shield by adding more leaves and flowers to the curved guide. Add the lines to the insides of the leaves in the top right compartment. Add the leaves to the plant in the compartment below it.

5

Erase the circle guide. Add more leaves and flowers to the wreath as shown. Lightly shade the banner beneath it and, looking at the photograph on the opposite page, add the shapes shown. Add as much detail as you like to the shield. You can finish your drawing with shading. Great job!

Jasmine

Pakistan made jasmine its national flower in 1954. Jasmine is a sweet-smelling blossom that is usually white or yellow. Its name comes from *yasmin*, a Persian word meaning "fragrant flower." Persia, now called Iran, ruled Pakistan in the sixth century B.C., when Pakistan was part of India.

Some botanists believe that jasmine originated in India. There the flower's leaves and buds are mixed with rice and eaten to help cure certain illnesses. The Mughal emperors who ruled Pakistan when it was part of India were very fond of jasmine and planted large groves of the flower in their gardens.

Today jasmine can be found almost anywhere in Pakistan. The Islamabad Rose and Jasmine Garden displays at least 12 different types of jasmine along with hundreds of kinds of roses. It is a popular place for tourists to visit.

1

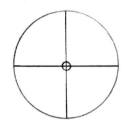

Draw a large circle. Draw a horizontal line across the circle's center. Draw a vertical line down its center. Add a small circle where the two lines meet.

2

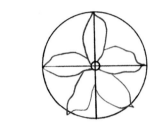

Draw five shapes for the petals, or parts of the flower, in the circle as shown. Notice how each one is slightly different in shape and size.

3

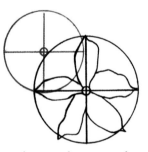

Repeat step 1, but make your shape smaller. Place it on the top left corner.

4

Erase the guidelines from the first circle and parts of the second. Add a jasmine flower in the second circle, as you did in the first. Notice where the petals overlap.

5

Erase the guidelines of the second circle. Draw thin lines in the shape of leaves behind the front flower. Notice how the leaves are long and thin at the top and bottom, and wider in the middle. Add the stems behind the leaves and flowers.

6

Finish your drawing by shading. You can make the shading in the smaller flower darker. Shade the leaves much darker than the flowers. You can use your finger to blend your pencil marks. Be sure to leave the stems and the edges of the leaves white as shown.

21

The Chukar Partridge

In 2001, Pakistan adopted the chukar partridge as its national bird. This was done to try to protect the wildlife that is disappearing in Pakistan.

Chukars are mostly gray, with a strip of black that runs from the eyes to below the neck. They also have black stripes on their sides. Both male and female chukars have bright red bills and legs. They live in rocky places, woodlands, and grasslands. There are 14 kinds of chukars that can be found not only in Pakistan, but also in Iran, Russia, China, Nepal, and the islands surrounding the Mediterranean Sea. Chukars are sometimes bred as game birds, which are birds that are hunted for sport. They are popular as game birds because they are easy to breed and there are large numbers of them.

1

Start by drawing a circle. This will be one of your guides to drawing the chukar partridge.

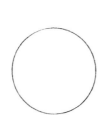

2

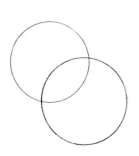

Draw another circle as shown. See how this circle crosses over the other circle. Notice too how it is slightly smaller than the first circle you drew.

3

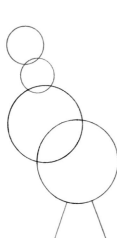

Draw two more smaller circles. Again, see how they cross over each other and the second circle you drew. Add two straight lines to the bottom circle. These are guides for the bird's legs.

4

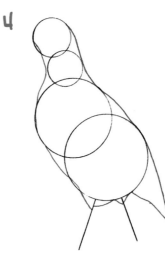

Connect the circles with wavy lines as shown. Follow closely the shape of the lines at the tail and at the bottom of the first circle.

5

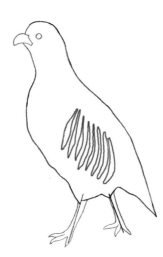

Erase the circles. Add the eye and the beak to the head. Erase the extra line where you drew the beak. Add shapes for the feathers as shown. Finish by drawing the legs and clawed feet.

6

Erase the straight leg guidelines. Erase extra lines. Finish by shading your drawing. Use dark and light shading. Notice that the shading is darker around the neck and eye area.

The Markhor

The markhor, a member of the goat family, is Pakistan's national animal. It was made the national animal in 2001, as part of an effort to preserve Pakistan's wildlife. The population of markhor has gotten smaller because many have been hunted. People like to hunt the markhor for its horns, which are long and curly. The markhor can weigh as much as 240 pounds (109 kg). The name "markhor" comes from the Persian words *mar*, meaning "snake," and *khor*, meaning "eating." Despite its name, however, the markhor does not eat snakes. It eats only grass and vegetables. It lives in dry, barren areas along the sides of cliffs or in the mountains. This animal can be found in Pakistan and in neighboring countries, such as Afghanistan and India.

1

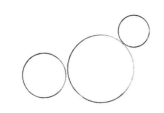

Draw three circles as shown. Notice how they are all different sizes, and the largest one is in the middle.

2

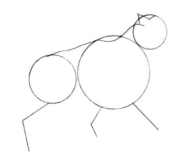

Connect the three circles at the top with a wavy line. Be sure to add a pointed shape for the markhor's ear. Add the lines coming from the two circles as shown.

3

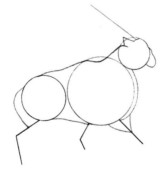

Draw an angled line coming from the top circle. Add the shape shown for the nose. Draw the lines around the body as shown.

4

Erase the front two circles. Add lines around the leg guidelines as shown. Draw the shape for the tail.

5

Erase the leg guidelines. Erase the remaining circle. Draw a curved line above the back leg. Add lines to the face for the hair. Draw a small line inside the ear. Add the eye and cheek lines. Add the shapes to the angled line you drew in step 3. This is the start of the markhor's horn.

6

Finish adding shapes to the horn. Add the fourth leg as shown. Draw lines for the hooves. Add lines for the nostril and the mouth.

7

Add dark and light shading. The markhor is very hairy, so draw shading lines that look like hair.

K2, Pakistan's Highest Mountain

Pakistan has some of the world's highest mountains. There are three separate mountain ranges in the country. They are the Himalayas, the Karakoram, and the Hindu Kush. Pakistan's tallest peak is K2. It reaches 28,250 feet (8,611 m), and is part of the Karakoram Range in the North. K2 stands on the border between northern Pakistan and western China. It is called K2 because it was the second peak of the Karakoram to be named. It is the world's second-highest mountain, after Mount Everest. In 1856, Colonel T. G. Montgomerie measured K2 for the British government. Pakistan at the time was a part of India and India was under British rule.

K2 is a very hard and dangerous mountain to climb. Many people have died trying to climb it. On July 31, 1954, Lino Lacedelli and Achille Compagnoni of Italy were the first people to reach the top of K2. The climb took them about two months.

1

Draw two large rectangles as shown. Make the bottom one slightly smaller.

2

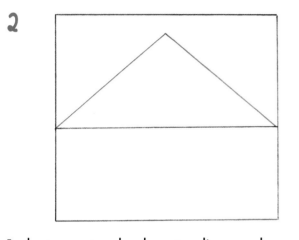

In the top rectangle, draw two lines as shown. These lines will make a triangle with the horizontal line you drew in step 1. This will be your guide for the mountaintop.

3

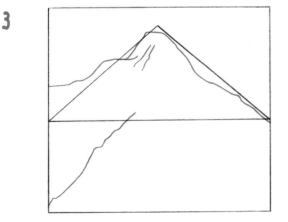

Draw the wavy line around the triangle guide as shown. Add the lines inside this shape. Draw a rough line coming from the bottom of the rectangle.

4

Erase the triangle. Add wavy lines for the clouds as shown. Add more rough lines to the right side of the mountain as shown.

5

Finish by shading the mountain. Notice that some of the ridges are dark. You can use your eraser to make white areas as shown. Well done! You have just drawn K2, Pakistan's tallest peak.

Mohenjo Daro

   Mohenjo Daro, in Sind province in southeastern Pakistan, was an ancient city built by the Dravidians around 2500 B.C. The city was part of the Indus Valley civilization. It was discovered during an archaeological dig in the 1920s. The dig shows that Mohenjo Daro was a well-planned city, with wide streets laid out neatly in grids. There were buildings such as markets, shops, baths, and houses. Each house had a courtyard, with a door on the side. Around the courtyard, there were rooms of different sizes, including a bathroom. The bathroom had drainage through which water flowed into street drains. The drainage system shows that the Dravidians were quite advanced in their building skills.

1

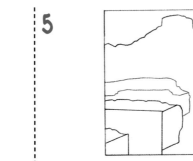

Start by drawing a rectangle. In the bottom half of the rectangle, draw a line that slopes from left to right as shown.

2

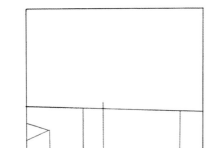

Draw vertical lines as shown. Add the shape in the bottom left corner. These lines will become walls at the front of Mohenjo Daro.

3

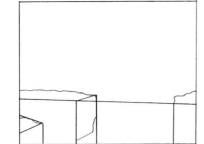

Add the lines as shown in the bottom section of the rectangle.

4

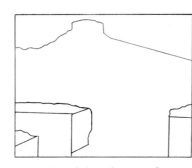

Erase the middle of the sloping line. Erase part of one of the vertical lines as shown. Erase the line at the top of the shape in the bottom left corner. At the top of the drawing, add a long wavy line to make the shape shown.

5

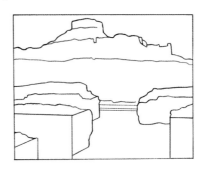

Draw the shapes at the top as shown. Add two more shapes at the middle section of the drawing. These will become more walls.

6

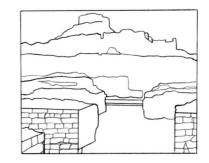

Erase the extra line at the top. Draw the three lines going across the top of the drawing as shown. Draw four rough lines between the two walls in the middle section.

7

Draw shapes for bricks on the front walls. Add lines and shapes to the other parts of the drawing as shown.

8

Finish by shading. Use light and dark shading as shown.

29

The Khyber Pass

The Khyber Pass is the most famous pass in the world. It is a steep, narrow, and winding passage between Afghanistan and Pakistan. It is 35 miles (56 km) long and is walled by cliffs. A stone gate marks the entrance to the Khyber Pass.

In the nineteenth century, when Britain ruled India, the British tried to control the Khyber Pass. The Afghans defended their border successfully until 1879, when the British took it over. The British controlled the pass until 1947, when they gave control to Pakistan. Today Pakistan continues to control the Khyber Pass. A railroad built by the British between 1920 and 1925 runs all the way to the Afghan border. There are 34 tunnels and 92 bridges along the pass.

1

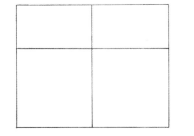

Start by drawing a rectangle. Draw a vertical line in the center of the rectangle. Next draw a horizontal line. Notice that this line is above the center. These lines make two small rectangles and two squares within the large rectangle.

2

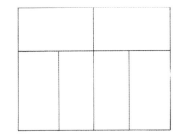

Draw two vertical lines as shown. Notice that the lines are slightly off center, making the rectangles at the sides a bit bigger.

3

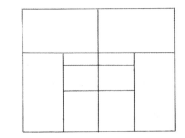

Draw two horizontal lines as shown.

4

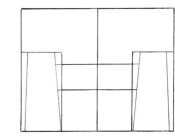

Erase the middle part of the top horizontal line. In the two rectangles on the sides, draw four sloping lines. These sloping lines will become the towers at the entrance to the Khyber Pass. Add small horizontal lines.

5

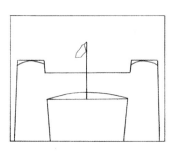

Erase the center vertical guideline, but leave part of it for the flagpole as shown. Add the shape for the flag. Erase the guidelines around the columns as shown. Draw a curved line from one tower to the other as shown. Draw a curved line at the top of each tower.

6

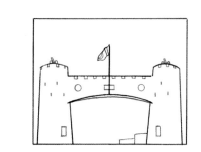

Erase the guidelines. Add rectangles and circles in the middle of the arch and on the columns. Add small lines and shapes to the rest of the gate. Add details to the flag as shown. Add lines to the top of the columns. These are cannons. Draw small shapes on the inside of the right column.

7

Erase extra lines. Finish by shading. Add lines across the columns as shown. You can use your finger to blend the shading. Well done! You have finished the entrance gate to the Khyber Pass.

Buddha Statue at Takht-i-Bahi

Buddhism is a religion based on the teachings of a holy man named Siddhārtha Gautama, also known as the Buddha. Buddhism began in northern India around 500 B.C. Buddhists believe in the search for enlightenment. The emperor Aśoka was a Buddhist. He ruled India in the third century B.C., when Pakistan was a part of India. Under his rule, Buddhism became popular and spread to central Asia and China.

One of the most popular symbols of Buddhism still standing in northern Pakistan today is the Takht-i-Bahi monastery in Gandhara. Gandhara was the center of Buddhism in India in ancient times. The ruins of Takht-i-Bahi include small shrines and rooms with niches, or cuts in the wall, for the monks' belongings. There are also statues of Buddha, carvings of scenes from his life, and other sculptures.

1

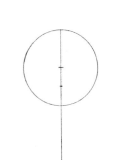

Draw a vertical line. Draw a large circle near the top. Draw two small horizontal lines on the first line. One is at the circle's center. One is between the center and the bottom edge.

2

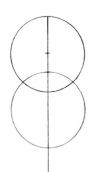

Draw another circle, the same size as the one you just drew. The top edge of the new circle begins on the lower horizontal line as shown.

3

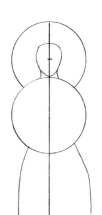

Add shapes for the neck and the head in the top circle as shown. Erase the bottom edge of the circle. Draw two curved lines coming from the second circle.

4

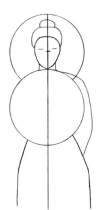

Draw a line on the right for the arm. Add shapes to the top of the head as shown. Draw two small lines for the eyes.

5

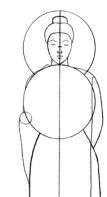

Add details such as the eyebrows, the nose, and the mouth to the face. Add lines to the body as shown. These are for the statue's robe. Add a circle where his hand will be.

6

Erase the vertical guideline. Erase the second circle and any extra lines. Add long shapes for the ears. Draw two dots on the eye lines. Draw a curved line for the robe's neckline. Add lines coming from the hand circle as shown.

7

Erase extra lines. Finish by adding shading. Notice that the shading is darker in some areas, such as the area behind the statue's head. Draw in some details, such as wavy lines in the hair and the robe.

Lahore Fort

 Southern Middle Media
5235 Solomon's Island Rd.
Lothian, MD 20711

During the 1500s, India, which included Pakistan, became part of the Mughal Empire. Bābur, a Muslim ruler from the central Asian country of Mongolia, was the first Mughal emperor. Bābur's descendant Akbar is considered the greatest Mughal emperor because he expanded the Mughal Empire and it flourished during his time. Akbar made Lahore in eastern Pakistan his capital from 1548 to 1598. He built Lahore Fort, also known as Shahi Qila, in 1566. The fort is a fine example of the grand architecture for which the Mughals were famous. Lahore Fort covers 30 acres (12 ha) of land. It includes palaces, halls, and gardens. The Alamgiri Gate is located on the western side of the fort. It was built in 1674 as a private entrance for the royal family. It was made large enough to allow elephants that carried the king or his family members to pass through.

1

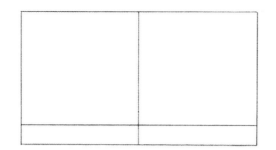

Draw a large rectangle as shown. Draw a vertical line down the center. Draw a horizontal line near the bottom as shown.

2

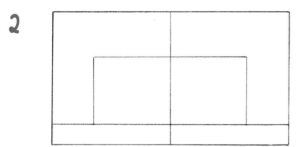

Draw more lines to make another rectangular shape. Make sure the sides are equal in length on both sides of the vertical line.

3

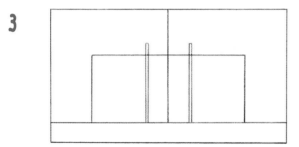

Erase the bottom part of the vertical guideline. Draw two long, skinny shapes on both sides of the vertical guideline.

4

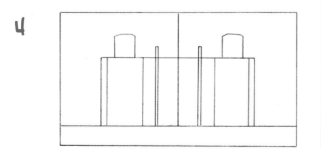

Draw more vertical lines as shown. Add two small shapes at the top of the rectangle. These are the beginning of the towers. Notice that the tops of these towers are curved instead of straight.

5

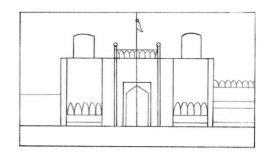

Draw a flag near the top of the vertical guideline. Draw a horizontal line near the top of the two skinny shapes. Add the shapes beneath it as shown. Draw little circles at the top of the two skinny shapes. Draw the shape for the doorway. Add lines and arches to the sides of the fort.

6

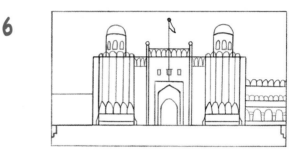

Erase any extra lines. Add domes to the tops of the towers at the sides. Draw windows and other lines inside the towers. Add long shapes at the sides of the fort. Add the details shown to the center of the fort, around the doorway. Draw more shapes on the right side of your drawing. Add the remaining lines below the bottom horizontal line.

7

Erase the extra lines. Add as much detail to your drawing as you like. Finish with shading. Notice that the shading inside the windows and doors is darker.

The Badshahi Mosque

Considered the last of the great Mughals, Emperor Aurangzeb ruled from 1658 to 1707. After he died in 1707, the Mughal Empire began to weaken. One of the things Aurangzeb is remembered for is the building of Badshahi Mosque in Lahore. A mosque is the place where Muslims go to pray. Badshahi, which was completed in 1676, is one of the biggest mosques in the world. It has huge gateways and three large domes. Its open courtyard can hold at least 60,000 people. It is believed that in one of the rooms above the entrance gate, which is closed to the public, hairs of Muhammad and the remains of some of his family members are kept. Muhammad was the founder of the Islamic faith. He was born in Mecca, Saudi Arabia, in A.D. 570. Pakistan was founded according to Islamic beliefs, and today Islam continues to unite Pakistanis, most of whom are Muslims.

1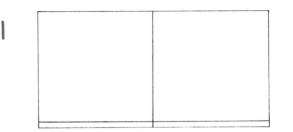

Draw a rectangle. Draw a vertical line down the center. Draw a horizontal line close to the bottom of the rectangle as shown.

2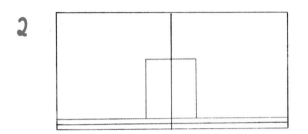

Draw another horizontal line. Draw three lines as shown, to make another rectangular shape.

3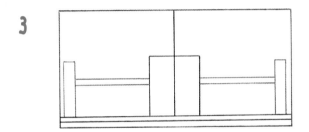

Erase the extra lines. Draw lines to make two thin rectangles near the right and left sides of the large rectangle. These will be towers. Draw horizontal lines connecting the thin rectangles to the center rectangle.

4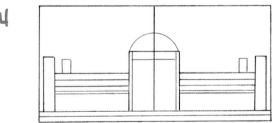

Add more horizontal lines. Draw more lines to make two small rectangular shapes on the top horizontal lines. These are also towers. In the central rectangle draw two vertical lines and one horizontal line. Draw a dome shape on top of the rectangle.

5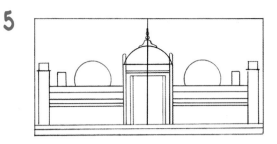

Add details to the dome as shown. Add more vertical and horizontal lines to the central rectangle. Draw two large curved shapes on the top horizontal line. Add lines to make two small rectangular shapes on the outermost towers.

6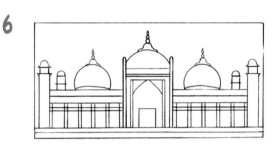

Erase the vertical line in the center. Add details to the central domed area. Add details to the large curved shapes. Draw small curved shapes on the tops of the four side towers. Add tiny lines to the outermost towers. Add horizontal lines to the other two towers. Draw vertical lines on both sides of the central area.

7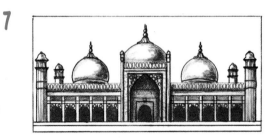

Add lines to the two side towers. Draw small arches across the bottom of the building. Add details, such as ovals and squiggly lines, to all areas of the mosque as shown. Finish by shading. Notice that the right sides of the domes and circles are dark.
The arches and doorway
are dark, too.

Derawar Fort

The Cholistan Desert in central Pakistan is the biggest desert in the country. The Hakra River used to run through this area, but it has dried up, leaving a vast desert. The people of Cholistan are nomads who herd and trade camels. At the edge of the desert is the Derawar Fort. This is the largest of all the forts in the area that protected a trade route stretching all the way to India. Nobody knows how old the original Derawar Fort is, but the fort that stands today was built in 1733 by the Abbasi family. The Abbasi family still owns the Derawar Fort today. It is a huge structure that can be seen from many miles (km) away. The fort is about 130 feet (40 m) high. It has 40 bastions, which are structures that were used for firing big guns.

1

Start by drawing a sloping line. It slopes upward from left to right. Draw two straight lines at a slight angle. These will be the sides for the first bastion.

2

Draw a wavy line at the bottom of the bastion. Draw a curved line that connects the two angled lines as shown. This is the top of the bastion.

3

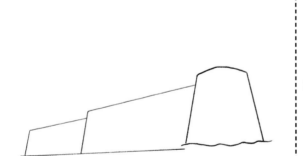

Erase the straight line beneath the wavy one you drew in step 2. Add the shapes shown. Notice how the lines are at a slight angle and that they curve slightly where they meet.

4

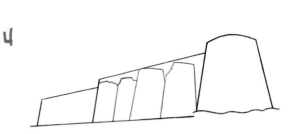

Draw four shapes within the first shape as shown. You have just drawn four more bastions. Notice that the lines at the tops of these bastions are not straight.

5

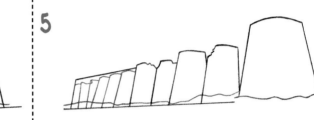

Add six more bastions in the second shape. You now have a total of eleven bastions. Draw a long wavy line across the bottom of ten of the bastions as shown. Erase the guidelines at the top of the first shape.

6

Erase the rest of the guidelines as shown. Add details to the tops of the bastions. Finish by shading. In some of the bastions, you can make the sides darker than the centers. You can use your finger to shade. Lightly shade the ground. Well done! You have drawn part of the Derawar Fort.

Tomb of Quaid-e-Azam

Mohammed Ali Jinnah is known in Pakistan as Quaid-e-Azam, or "the great leader." He was given the name because he united his people and founded Pakistan. Jinnah was born in 1876, to a middle-class Muslim family in Karachi, when Pakistan was a part of India. In 1913, he joined the Muslim League, a group fighting for self-government in India. In the 1930s, the Muslim League began to demand a homeland for Muslims in India. In 1935, Jinnah became the leader of the Muslim League. In 1947, both the Hindus and the British government accepted Pakistan's separation from India. Jinnah became the first governor-general of an independent Pakistan. He died in 1948, just one year after Pakistan's independence. Today Jinnah's tomb in Karachi is one of Pakistan's most popular monuments. The marble tomb is on a hill in a park and was planned by Yahya C. Merchant. It was built in the 1970s.

1

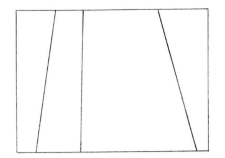

Draw a rectangle. Add three sloping lines as shown.

2

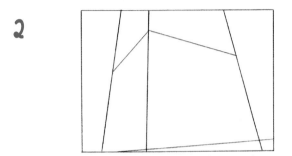

Add more sloping lines. Two of these lines should be toward the top of the drawing. These will be the top edges of the tomb. The third one is very close to the bottom.

3

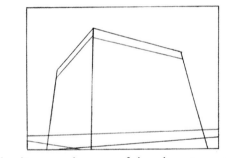

Erase the lines at the top of the drawing. Add two more lines along the top edges of the tomb as shown. Draw two sloping lines near the bottom.

4

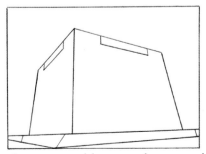

Draw four short vertical lines at the top edges of the tomb. Erase parts of the horizontal lines on either side of these lines. Erase the small lines at the bottom of the tomb. Draw three short sloping lines at the bottom.

5

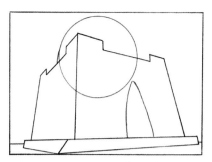

Erase extra lines. Draw two short horizontal lines. Draw the shape for the doorway at the front of the tomb as shown. Add a large circle and a small line coming from the circle.

6

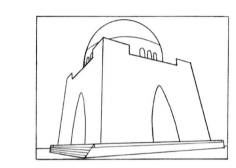

Erase the bottom part of the circle. You have just drawn a dome. Draw curved lines in the dome as shown. Add details for windows in the dome. Draw lines for the steps. Draw another doorway at the left side of the building.

7

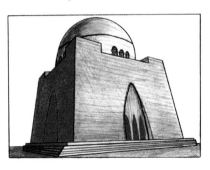

Add more lines to finish the steps. Erase any extra lines. Draw light lines across the front of the tomb, shading it lightly. Shade in three small arching doors within the large doorway at the front. Finish the tomb by shading. Press hard to make darker shading and lightly to make light shading. Make the left side of the tomb and part of the dome darker.

Minar-e-Pakistan

The tower Minar-e-Pakistan, or Pakistan Day Memorial, rises above the Iqbal Park in Lahore. Standing about 197 feet (60 m) high, the tower is made of concrete, stone, and marble. It was built in 1960. Its base platform, which is shaped like a five-pointed star, encloses crescent-shaped pools. The crescent and the star are traditional symbols of Islam.

The tower was built in honor of the signing of the Pakistan Resolution on March 23, 1940. In this resolution, the Muslim League made demands for a separate homeland for Muslims in India. The tower was built at the place where the Muslim League met in 1940. At the meeting, Mohammed Ali Jinnah said Hindus and Muslims in India belonged to two different religions with different customs. He said to insist on putting them together in one nation would lead only to unhappiness. The people of Pakistan celebrate March 23 as their national holiday.

1

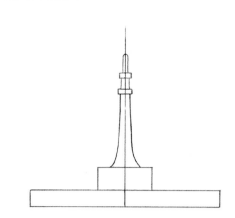

Start by drawing a horizontal line. Add a long vertical line at its center. These are guidelines for drawing the Pakistan Day Memorial tower.

2

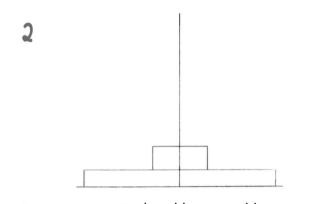

Draw more vertical and horizontal lines as shown. These lines make two rectangular shapes. The bottom rectangle is long and thin. The top one is shorter and wider.

3

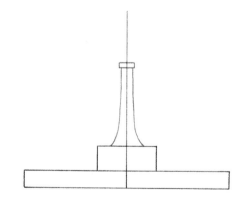

Draw two curved lines next to the vertical line. Draw a small rectangle at the top of the lines.

4

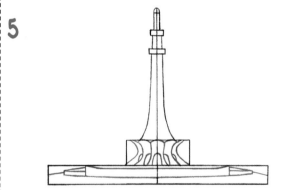

Add three more shapes on top of the shape you have just drawn. Notice that the highest one is rounded at the top.

5

Erase the vertical line above the shapes you just drew. Add details at the bottom of the tower as shown. Draw a small horizontal line at the top.

6

Erase the guidelines. Add a small vertical line to the top of the tower. Finish the tower by shading. The tower has a lot of small areas of dark shading that look like windows. You can make the right side of the tower darker than the left. Shade in the step areas.

43

Timeline

2500 B.C.	The Dravidians settle in the Indus Valley.
1700 B.C.	The Aryans from central Asia settle in Pakistan.
500 B.C.	Persian emperor Cyrus controls part of Pakistan.
A.D. 1206	Most of Pakistan is under the Delhi Sultanate, a Muslim empire in India.
1526	Bābur invades India and Pakistan and founds the Mughal Empire.
1600s	European countries trade with the Mughal Empire.
1857	The United Kingdom takes control of India.
1800s–1900s	Hindus and Muslims in India ask the British government for self-government.
1906	The Muslim League in India is founded.
1940	The Muslim League demands a homeland for Muslims in India, called Pakistan.
1947	Pakistan becomes independent.
1971	East Pakistan separates from Pakistan and becomes Bangladesh. General Yahya Khan resigns as president. He is replaced by Zulfikar Ali Bhutto.
1979	Bhutto is executed after being found guilty of ordering the killing of a politician.
1988	Benazir Bhutto becomes prime minister and the first woman to lead a Muslim country.
2001	Pakistanis vote to let General Pervez Musharraf serve as Pakistan's president for five years.

Pakistan Fact List

Official Name	Islamic Republic of Pakistan
Area	307,374 square miles (796,095 sq km)
Population	148,000,000
Capital	Islamabad, population, 901,137
Most-Populated City	Karachi, population, 14,000,000
Industries	Textiles and clothing, food products, fertilizer, steel, cement
Agriculture	Wheat, cotton, rice, sugarcane, milk, chickpeas
National Flower	Jasmine
National Tree	Deodar
National Bird	Chukar partridge
National Anthem	"Pak Sarzamin Shad Bad" ("Blessed Be the Sacred Land")
Language	Urdu is the national language, but more than 300 dialects are spoken in Pakistan.
Highest Mountain Peak	K2, 28,250 feet (8,611 m)
Longest River	Indus River, 1,800 miles (2,897 km)
National Holiday	March 23, Republic Day

Glossary

archaeological (ar-kee-uh-LA-jih-kul) Having to do with the study of the way humans lived long ago.

Aryans (A-ree-unz) People who came to the Indus Valley from central Asia.

bastions (BAS-chunz) Works of earth, brick, or stone that stand out from a secured building.

Buddhism (BOO-dih-zum) A faith based on the teachings of Buddha, started in India.

crescent (KREH-sent) Something that is shaped like a curved moon.

cultural (KUL-chuh-rul) Having to do with the beliefs and practices of a group of people.

customs (KUS-tumz) Practices common to many people in an area or a social class.

dangerous (DAYN-jer-us) Able to cause harm.

declared (dih-KLERD) Announced officially.

demanded (dih-MAN-ded) Appealed or ordered.

demonstration (deh-mun-STRAY-shun) A public display or gathering for a person or a cause.

descendant (dih-SEN-dent) A person who is born of a certain family or group.

dialects (DY-uh-lekts) Different ways that a language is spoken in different areas.

discipline (DIH-sih-plin) Training or developing by teaching and exercise.

drainage (DRAY-nij) A system that causes a lessening in amount, content, or power.

emblem (EM-blum) A sign or figure that stands for something.

enlightenment (en-LY-ten-ment) A state of knowing more than ever before.

executed (EK-suh-kyoot-ed) Put to death.

expanded (ek-SPAND-ed) Spread out, or grew larger.

fort (FORT) A strong building or place that can be defended against an enemy.

founded (FOWN-did) Started.

fragrant (FRAY-grint) Having a smell.

grids (GRIDZ) Patterns of evenly spaced lines running up, down, and across.

heritage (HER-ih-tij) The stories and ways of doing things that are passed from parent to child.

Hinduism (HIN-doo-ih-zum) A faith that was started in India.

holy (HOH-lee) Blessed; important for reasons of faith.

independent (in-dih-PEN-dent) Free from the control or support of other people.

industries (IN-dus-treez) Businesses in which many people work and make money producing a particular product.

invaders (in-VAYD-erz) People who attack a place in order to take it over.

involved (in-VOLVD) Kept busy by something.

Islamic (is-LAH-mik) Having to do with a faith based on the teachings of Muhammad and the Koran.

monastery (MAH-nuh-ster-ee) A house where people who have taken vows of faith live and work.

motto (MAH-toh) A phrase that stands for something or that states what someone believes.

nomadic (noh-MA-dik) Describing a person who moves from place to place.

petroleum (peh-TROH-lee-um) An oily liquid that can be used to make gasoline and other products.

prime minister (PRYM MIH-nih-ster) The leader of a government.

prosperity (prah-SPER-ih-tee) The condition of being successful.

rejected (ree-JEKT-ed) Turned down something; refused.

remains (rih-MAYNZ) The parts left after a living thing has died.

resigns (rih-ZYNZ) Steps down from a position.

resolution (reh-zuh-LOO-shun) A formal statement adopted by a group of people.

ruins (ROO-enz) Old, falling-down buildings.

shrines (SHRYNZ) Special places built in honor of important people.

symbols (SIM-bulz) Objects or pictures that stand for something else.

textiles (TEK-stylz) Woven fabric or cloth.

tomb (TOOM) A grave.

tourists (TUR-ists) People who take a trip for pleasure.

traditional (truh-DIH-shuh-nul) Usual; done in a way that has been passed down over time.

unity (YOO-nih-tee) Togetherness.

Index

Web Sites

Due to the changing nature of Internet links, PowerKids Press has developed an online list of Web sites related to the subject of this book. This site is updated regularly. Please use this link to access the list:
www.powerkidslinks.com/kgdc/pakistan/